SPIDERS

Text by Sarah Lovett

John Muir Publications
Santa Fe, New Mexico

Very special thanks to
Sandy Brantley, Technician, Department of Biology, University of New Mexico

John Muir Publications, P.O. Box 613, Santa Fe, New Mexico 87504

© 1991 by John Muir Publications
All rights reserved. Published 1991
Printed in the United States of America

First edition. Sixth printing September 1994
                Second TWG printing December 1993

Library of Congress Cataloging-in-Publication Data
Lovett, Sarah, 1953—
    Extremely weird spiders   /   text by Sarah Lovett.
      p. cm.
    Summary : Text and photos introduce unusual spiders.
    Softcover ISBN 1-56261-007-4
    Hardcover ISBN 1-56261-177-1
    1. Spiders—Juvenile literature. [1. Spiders.] I. Title.
QL458.4.L68 1991   91-9879
595.4'4—dc20   CIP
                                    AC

Extremely Weird Logo Art: Peter Aschwanden
Illustrations: Mary Sundstrom, Sally Blakemore
Design: Sally Blakemore
Typography: Copygraphics, Santa Fe, New Mexico
Printer: Guynes Printing, Albuquerque, New Mexico
Bindery: Prizma Industries, Inc.

Distributed to the book trade by
W. W. Norton & Co., Inc.
New York, New York

Distributed to the education market by
Wright Group Publishing, Inc.
19201 120th Avenue N.E.
Bothell, Washington 98011-9512

Cover photo, hunting spider feeding on a katydid
(Courtesy Animals Animals © Michael Fogden)

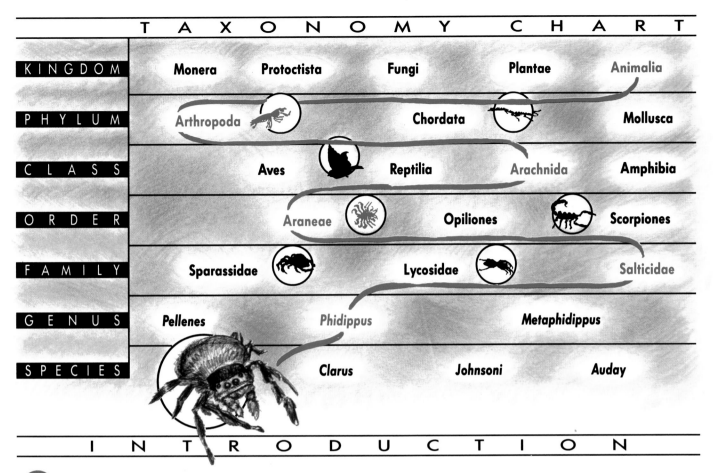

KINGDOM	Monera	Protoctista	Fungi	Plantae	Animalia
PHYLUM	Arthropoda		Chordata		Mollusca
CLASS	Aves		Reptilia	Arachnida	Amphibia
ORDER	Araneae		Opiliones		Scorpiones
FAMILY	Sparassidae		Lycosidae		Salticidae
GENUS	Pellenes	Phidippus		Metaphidippus	
SPECIES		Clarus	Johnsoni	Auday	

I N T R O D U C T I O N

Spiders are invertebrates, which means they don't have backbones. Ninety percent of all animal species on earth are invertebrates. These small creatures help plants reproduce by pollinating them. They also help recycle dead trees and animals back into the earth. And they are a vital source of food for birds, fish, and small mammals. Without invertebrates, like spiders and insects, many other living things would not survive.

Spiders belong to a group of "joint-legged" animals. They don't have antennae or wings, but they do have four pairs of legs and a hard outer shell, or exoskeleton. (Mammals like us, in contrast, have internal skeletons.) Most spiders live only one or two years, but some (like female tarantulas) set records at 20 years. Spiders can be found almost anywhere in the world, but they are most plentiful in tropical areas.

Spiders usually have eight eyes, variously arranged on their faces, and some have very sharp sight. All spiders have two main body parts—the cephalothorax and the abdomen. All legs attach to the cephalothorax. That is also where the brain, poison glands, and stomach are located. The heart, respiratory and reproductive organs, digestive tract, and silk glands are all found in the abdomen.

Spiders are famous for their silky skills. Some spin complex webs; some only use a single dragline or safety line. Most spiders make silken egg sacs to protect their young. And one orb weaver makes a silk that is the strongest natural fiber in the world!

Scientists use a universal system to keep track of spiders and the millions of animal and plant species on earth. That system is called taxonomy, and it starts with the 5 main (or broadest) groups of all living things, the kingdoms. It then divides those into the next groups down—phylum (animals with backbones all belong to the phylum chordata), then class, order, family, genus, and, finally, species. Members of a *species* look similar, and they can reproduce with each other. More than 35,000 of the earth's spider species have been named so far. Scientists guess there are many more, perhaps over 100,000, that haven't been named yet!

For an example of how taxonomy works, follow the highlighted lines above to see how the jumping spider, *Phidippus clarus*, is classified. In this book, the scientific family of each spider is listed next to the common name.

Turn to the glossarized index at the back of this book if you're looking for a specific spider, or for special information (what's molting, for instance), or for the definition of a word you don't understand.

Lucky Shamrock

To see the spider spin a web, flip the pages.

SHAMROCK SPIDER (Family: Araneidae)

The shamrock—named for a clover-shaped spot on its abdomen—might be a lucky spider. Part of a large group called orb weavers, shamrock spiders are often busy spinning nifty circular webs between bushes and vines and tall grasses throughout North America.

Female shamrocks reach sizes of a half-inch. Males are much smaller—one-fifth of an inch. Both are famous for spinning amazing geometric webs in a step-by-step process. First, a basic scaffold of mooring lines is set down by the spider. Then, the radial lines, like bicycle spokes, are added. Finally, the spider begins the circular pattern, working from the inside out to the largest circumference.

Young orb weavers don't go to school to learn weaving; instead, they follow their instincts. With no training from adult spiders, even the tiniest, freshly hatched spiderling knows how to spin silk and weave webs.

MARY SUNDSTROM

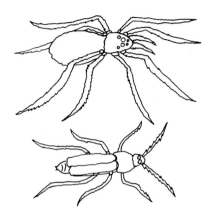

Spiders are not insects. There are many differences between the two, but the most obvious is that spiders have eight walking legs while insects only have six. Insects also have one pair of antenna and often have wings, but spiders have none.

Spiders, scorpions, mites, sea spiders, insects, crustaceans, and horseshoe crabs all belong to the same scientific phylum, Arthropoda. Together, they make up more than 900,000 species. Arachnids are arthropods who have four pairs of legs and no wings. They number about 70,000 species. A single group of arachnids, spiders, boast a mere 35,000 species.

SALLY BLAKEMORE

SPIDERS

GIANT WOLF SPIDER (Family: Lycosidae)

Giant wolf spiders are wonderfully hairy, and their eyes are very big, all eight of them! Four smallish eyes are set low on the spider's face, a large pair of eyes sits above them and points straight ahead, while farther back, two big eyes look up like tiny searchlights. This eye design means the wolf spider can see in four directions at once and spy moving creatures at a distance of 3 to 4 inches. That's a pretty long way for spiders.

All wolf spiders are excellent hunters. They are fast and strong, pouncing on victims and then crushing and biting them.

The bodies of giant wolf spiders grow to lengths of one and one-half inches, and these ground-dwelling creatures can be found almost anywhere in the world—they're not fussy about where they set up house.

Female wolf spiders are devoted mothers who wrap their eggs in a silken sac that they drag along with them everywhere. After about three weeks, spiderlings emerge when the female bites open the sac. These tiny spiders climb onto their mother's back, and there they stay for a week while she hunts and even battles other creatures. Spider babies must cling tight for the ride or they will be left behind. After the spiderlings molt (shed their outer skin), they are ready to begin a hunter's life on their own.

Spiders don't eat dinner, they drink it. After catching prey, spiders inject venom to paralyze the victim. They then regurgitate digestive juices over the prey so that it becomes liquid and drinkable. Sometimes, spiders start "drinking" before their victim is dead.

Why are all those weird people dancing the tarantella? In the 1500s and 1600s, big European wolf spiders were wrongly blamed for causing the nervous disease, "tarantism." Once bitten, people supposedly began dancing wildly, the only cure. Actually, the bite of a European wolf spider is harmless. History buffs still wonder what caused all the fuss? It could have been another spider, but, more likely, some people's imaginations got carried away. Or, maybe they just felt like dancing.

SPIDERS

GREEN LYNX SPIDER (Family: Oxyopidae)

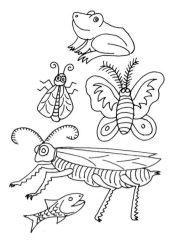

Named for the shiny bright color of its body, the green lynx spider is bedecked with tiny red spots, red knee joints, and rows and rows of black spines on all eight legs. Lynx legs are made for jumping—from stem to stem and leaf to leaf. These sturdy spiders spend most of their lives on plants, hunting in the day using their very sharp eyes. Lynx spiders are not in the habit of weaving webs. Instead, they trail a dragline, tacking it to leaves and twigs as they travel in search of prey.

A mother green lynx spider carefully binds her straw-colored egg sac to a nest of silk and twigs close to home. There, she wraps her legs around the sac and hangs head first, waiting patiently for her spiderlings to hatch.

Just one of many species of lynx spiders found around the world, the green lynx lives in the southern United States, Mexico, and Central America.

As part of the food chain, spiders dine on flies, moths, beetles, and other insects. Some spiders even eat frogs and fish! Tiny spiderlings must leave the egg sac before they begin to eat each other. To keep things in balance, lizards, birds, and insects are major predators of spiders.

Spiders use a dragline as their safety line. As they travel, this strand of silk plays out behind them. They tack it to twigs, leaves, or to anything handy. This way, if they fall, they only fall as far as the end of the line.

Photo, facing page, courtesy Animals Animals © K.G. Preston-Mafham

SPIDERS

BLACK WIDOW (Family: Theridiidae)

Around the world, there is a group of shiny black spiders recognized by their bright red markings and feared for their venom that attacks the nervous system.

In some areas, they are commonly called black wolf spiders, hourglass spiders, and shoe-button spiders. In North America, this spider goes by the name of black widow, and the female is one of the most poisonous of all spiders.

Although the black widow has a scary reputation, she's actually very shy and passive, hunting only for food. She likes to build her web in, on, or close to the ground where it will snag passing insects. When the black widow feels someone tugging on the web, she comes out of hiding and approaches with care.

Using her hind legs, she draws fresh silk from her spinnerets and binds up the struggling victim. Now, the spider is ready to inject her venom by piercing the victim's leg with her minute, needle-sharp fangs. While the insect still struggles, the black widow begins to hoist it into the air with her silken system of pulleys, until it finally reaches a height of three inches. Then, the victim can be moved to a convenient place deep in the spider's maze. Feasting for three or four days, the spider eventually sucks her prey dry until only a shell remains to be tossed away somewhere inside the mazelike web.

Although the black widow only bites humans when she feels her life is threatened, her bite is very dangerous. Learn to be on the look-out for this spider in wood piles and under rocks.

Spider silk is truly amazing. Some spider webs, stretched into a single line, would reach for more than 300 miles. Although webs are an important part of a spider's life, these tiny critters also use silk to drift on air currents at altitudes of 2,500 feet, to protect their eggs, and even to flirt! Male spiders pluck out a rhythm on the strings of a female's web to win her favor.

Photo, facing page, courtesy Animals Animals © Raymond A. Mendez

SPIDERS

HAIRY TARANTULA (Family: Theraphosidae)

When they need to grow, all spiders do it the hard way—shedding their outer too-tight skeleton (or cuticle) in exchange for a whole new suit of clothes—in a process called "molting." Although molting is risky and dangerous for spiders, they have no say in the matter. It's part of their natural behavior. But it is the time they are most vulnerable to their enemies.

The biggest American tarantulas usually begin this risky business in late summer. They refuse to eat and become very sloowww. Their bodies look dull and worn out because they're sporting last year's hairy skin.

Tarantulas spend several hours spinning a special molting bed, a soft sheet of silk, to lie on. With front and hind legs attached to the bed and lying on their backs, the spider looks almost dead. It takes two or three hours before the old cuticle begins to split along the sides and back of the spider's body. Then, rhythmical cramps help the spider pull its new legs from their old case—front legs first. In a shiny new cuticle (complete with a full set of hairs), the tarantula now lies quietly for two to three hours to toughen up. While this fresh cuticle is still soft, the spider can grow noticeably in size.

Within the spider community, the number of molts depends on the size of the spider. The smallest spiders only molt five or six times. Male tarantulas sometimes molt more than 20 times in their life, and females claim the record at 30 or 40 times! Most spiders stop molting once they reach sexual maturity, but tarantulas are long lived and primitive as spiders go, so they molt even after they're fully grown.

Arthropods don't have skeletons inside their bodies. Instead, they're encased in a hard outer shell. Because this outer skeleton doesn't grow, spiders and other arthropods must shed their skeleton suit from time to time, in order to increase their size. This process is called "molting."

Molting spiders are hard to find because they try to molt in private, very protected places.

SPIDERS

GOLDENROD SPIDER (Family: Thomisidae)

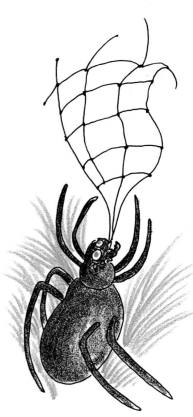

The goldenrod spider might not be showing its true colors, because it's actually white! The truth is, this pretty spider changes color from white to yellow depending on the flowers in the background. Goldenrod spiders (and other varieties of flower spiders) spend most of their lives in the heads of flowers. There, they lie in wait ready to ambush flying insects that are in search of flower nectar.

Big, fierce bugs—bees, wasps, large-winged butterflies—are captured by these pygmy ambushers.

Scientists have discovered that flying insects avoid light-colored blossoms that have dark spots resembling spiders. If they want to catch dinner, flower spiders must color-coordinate with their background. Goldenrod spiders are masters of camouflage; in one week's time, they can turn from white to yellow. In 4 or 5 days, they can return to white. This ability allows them to hunt from either yellow or white blossoms.

Spiders secrete a sticky mucous that they "glue" onto certain areas of their web. After a day or two, this glue is no longer sticky, so the spider eats its web and spins a brand-new one from scratch.

Photo, facing page, courtesy Animals Animals © Breck P. Kent

SPIDERS

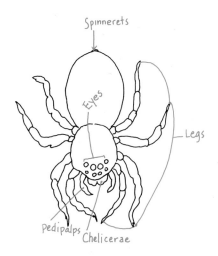

WATER SPIDER (Family: Argyronetidae)

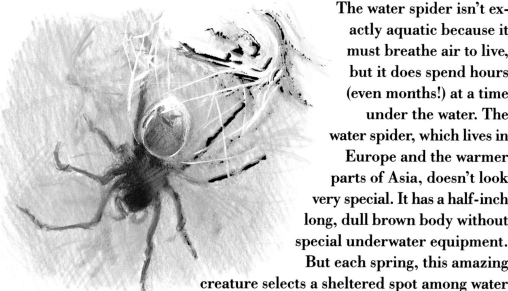

The water spider isn't exactly aquatic because it must breathe air to live, but it does spend hours (even months!) at a time under the water. The water spider, which lives in Europe and the warmer parts of Asia, doesn't look very special. It has a half-inch long, dull brown body without special underwater equipment.

But each spring, this amazing creature selects a sheltered spot among water plants below the surface of quiet streams and ponds. There, it spins a platform of silk anchored to plants. After rising to the surface, it lifts its abdomen to catch an air bubble and, hind legs stiff, paddles down below the silk platform to release the bubble. The air is then trapped underneath the silk, bubble after bubble, until a tiny diving bell is created. In this bell, the water spider eats, molts, mates, and raises a family.

During the mating season, a male diving spider spins his smaller diving bell next door to the female. The two homes are connected by a silken tunnel. The spider's eggs mature inside an egg sac attached to the upper part of the chamber. In three weeks, the spiderlings emerge, expert swimmers from birth.

In the fall, water spiders construct their winter homes in deeper water. This time, their home is a closed sac, often spun inside an empty snail shell. There, during the winter months, the spider stays dormant with enough air to survive until warmer weather.

Spiders have eight legs plus two chelicerae and two pedipalps. What are all these appendages for? *Chelicerae* are the very first appendages on the spider's head. They look like pincers, and they have fangs to inject venom into prey. The *pedipalps* are the second pair of appendages, and they are used to locate and crush prey. Next come four pairs of legs. Finally, *spinnerets* are tiny appendages on the spider's rear end. Silk is spun through these.

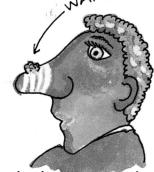

In medieval times, some people believed that a spider's web used as a band-aid would cure a wart.

Photo, facing page, courtesy Animals © OSF

SPIDERS

JUMPING SPIDER (Family: Salticidae)

This massive and hairy critter is a jumpy member of the largest group of American jumping spiders. With brightly colored bodies, curly beards, and bands of shimmering scales, jumping spiders are rainbow bright. They can be especially proud of their stylish legs, fringed with plumes of red, orange, or yellow hairs.

Male jumping spiders use their front legs to charm females during the mating season. Almost dancing, they sway and sashay in a zigzag pattern designed to show off the glory of their plumes and the iridescent gleam of their scales. Male charm is especially important because female jumping spiders are known for their bad tempers. Approaching and retreating with their dance steps, male spiders must time their courting techniques perfectly, or they could end up as the female's dinner instead of her mate.

Most spiders mate once a year when the weather is warmest, but they can produce more than one egg sac per mating. Indeed, true spiders have a life span of only one or two years, so they may only mate twice in a lifetime.

Spiders have a nifty way of moving to new locations—via silken parachutes. From a high blade of grass, flower, or fence post, the spider stands on the tips of its legs, abdomen toward the sky. From the spinnerets, many silken strands travel up on air currents until they are buoyant enough to lift the spider up, up, and away (sometimes as high as 5,000 feet). Spiders are known to travel hundreds of miles by "ballooning." In this way, they pioneer new habitats. Of course, ballooning has a down side: spiders never know where they will land!

Jumping spiders are eight-legged athletes able to leap ten inches at a time. If you were an extremely big (and weird) jumping spider, you could jump 40 feet!

SPIDERS

MEXICAN RED KNEE TARANTULA (Family: Theraphosidae)

Big, hairy mygalomorphs (a.k.a. tarantulas) are the whoppers of all spiders. Nicknamed "hairy spiders," tarantulas have a ferocious reputation that's really undeserved. Although a few tropical species are very poisonous, most tarantulas are nearly harmless to humans. These giants are really easygoing critters that only attack if threatened or pushed to extremes. Even then, although their bite can be painful, the effects are about the same as a bee sting.

Most tarantulas are ground-dwelling creatures that live in the same burrow for life, which means as long as thirty years for female tarantulas. These spiders may dig their own home or fix up a burrow abandoned by rodents. Each tarantula's hunting ground will only reach as far as a few feet to either side of its front door. So when it is frightened, it can easily rush back into the safety of home.

A loose web of silk over the entrance of a tarantula's burrow means the spider is back at home after a night's hunt. During cold winter months, the burrow's opening might be stuffed with silk, bits of leaves, and earth. This helps keep them warm, and it also discourages unwelcome visitors.

FANG

Some spiders are true, while others are primitive. Actually, primitive spiders include tarantulas, trap-door spiders, and a few relatives. Generally, they're big, their fangs point back, and they all use the same hunting method. True spiders have developed fangs that are "cross-eyed" and much easier to use; they also have many special ways of hunting. Primitive and true spiders are different, but one is not better than the other.

Most mygalomorphs are big hairy creatures—the group includes tarantulas, trap-door spiders, and their other kin.

SPIDERS

FISHING SPIDER (Family: Pisauridae)

Big-eyed fishing spiders are pond-skaters, able to skim over the water's surface because their bodies are extremely light compared to their size. Tiny hairs, sticky and plentiful on their legs, also help provide buoyancy and traction when skating. Because they are balloon light, fishing spiders can't dive or stay underwater unless they attach themselves to leaves. Like many spiders, fishing spiders can use an air bubble for underwater breathing—but only for a very short time.

True to their name, sharp-eyed fishing spiders are known to catch very small minnows and tadpoles for dinner. Their system is to perch their two back legs on a small stone, rock, or twig and cast their other six legs out over the water. When a tadpole cruises by, the fishing spider plunges suddenly underwater and wraps its legs around the startled prey. After a great struggle, the tadpole is lugged back onto the perch and devoured.

Spiders live in almost every nook and cranny of the world, below ground and above. Indeed, spiders have been found above altitudes of 20,000 feet on Mount Everest.

Photo, facing page, courtesy Animals Animals © Alastair MacEwen/OSF

SPIDERS

CRAB SPIDER (Family: Thomisidae)

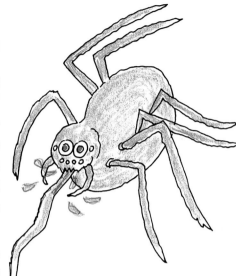

All spiders can lose a leg or two without feeling the pinch. This ability is called "autotomy," and it comes in handy to escape tricky situations—especially when somebody else wants to eat you for dinner. Mature spiders must do without lost limbs, but young spiders (those still molting) can regrow legs that work almost like new.

Nimble crab spiders can manage minus one, two, or even three legs and still escape the clutches of an enemy on the run. Since front legs in crab spiders are important organs of touch as well as weapons of attack, catching flies is a real problem without them. When both front legs are left behind, crab spiders simply aim the next pair in a forward direction.

In order to autotomize a leg, spiders need something to push against. When a predator grabs a spider by one leg, that leg will snap loose at its weakest point if the spider is able to hold onto a twig or a leaf. If the spider is held in the air, it must push itself away from the predator or it won't be able to lose its leg and escape to safety.

If a spider is bitten by a predator that only breaks the cuticle of a leg, the spider will probably bleed to death. To save its life, a spider instinctually amputates the wounded leg. To do this, it uses its mouth and other legs to pull the leg off, or it spins threads attached to its leg and pulls against them. After amputation, spiders suck the leg dry.

Sticky, tacky hairs on spiders' feet keep them from slipping and sliding when they land after a jump. These hairs are also handy for scaling slick surfaces.

Photo, facing page, courtesy Animals Animals © Richard Shiell

SPIDERS

BLACK AND YELLOW GARDEN SPIDER (Family: Araneidae)

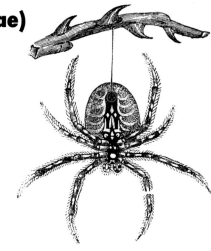

The plump black and yellow garden spider spins her two-foot-wide web over shrubs, flowers, and other handy garden plants. Even in a heat wave, she can be found perched proudly in the center of her webby kingdom like a black and yellow bull's-eye. Grasshoppers are a favorite meal, although a variety of flying insects whizz in for dinner. Like many garden spiders, the black and yellow is a skilled spinner, and she uses her silk for several jobs. Besides building her home and hunting, this spider deposits her eggs inside a soft silken sac and hangs it from a nearby shrub. Silk is a spider's all-purpose tool.

Spider silk is extremely amazing stuff. A super protein produced as a liquid in special silk glands located in the spider's abdomen, silk hardens as it is stretched from the spinnerets. Spider silk might look delicate, but the relative tension needed to break it is far greater than for steel. And there's more than one type of silk. The spider uses non-stick silk for radial web lines and sticky silk for the spiraling circles. Also, some silk is ultraviolet to attract insects.

Spiders are as old as the hills. In fact, they are some of the earliest of earth's land predators, dating back at least 380 million years. Scientists can keep their dates straight because a fossil spinneret —no bigger than a pin head—was recently discovered in New York state. Of course, we all know that spinnerets are teensy raised openings found on a spider's rear end. Through these openings, liquid spider silk becomes the stuff webs are made of.

Photo, facing page, courtesy Animals Animals © Charlie Palek

SPIDERS

OGRE-FACED STICK SPIDER (Family: Dinopidae)

With two out of eight eyes like giant head-lamps, stiltlike legs, a humped body that could pass for a thorn, a twig, or a bud, and an odd head, the ogre-faced stick spider looks extremely weird. But looks aren't everything, and this spider is famed for casting its silky "net" over flying prey. For this reason, some people call it the net-casting spider.

Ogre-faced stick spiders spend their days pressed flat against the bark of a tree limb with their front legs stretched out and their back legs holding firm around the branch. This strange perch makes it very hard for passing predators to spot them. But after sundown, it's another story.

The ogre-faced spider begins each evening's work by first spinning a small rectangular net about the size of a postage stamp. The spider holds the little net with its four front legs and uses its back legs to hang onto the main web. Hanging downward, ogre-face waits for the right moment to cast itself forward, with its net stretched 5 or 6 times normal size to catch a passing insect. The unfortunate prey is instantly paralyzed with spider venom, then wrapped in silk and eaten. This same method and net are used all night. When the ogre-faced spider is full, or daylight arrives, it neatly rolls its net into a ball and drops it to the ground.

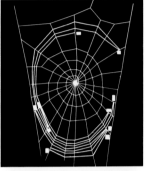

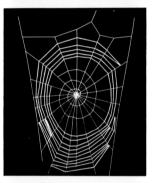

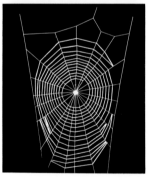

Models showing the process of weaving the web of *Eperia sericata* (*sclopellaria*) (Neg. No. 37859; Photo R.C. Lenskjold; Courtesy Department Library Services, American Museum of Natural History)

Step into my parlor, said the spider to the fly. Why do bugs fly into spider webs? Maybe they really are invited. Scientists have recently discovered that some spiders decorate their webs with silk strands that reflect ultraviolet light. And, what do you know, webs with ultraviolet strands attract more bugs than webs without. Apparently, for bugs, ultraviolet light is a sign of the clear blue sky.

SPIDERS

Photo, facing page, courtesy Animals Animals © OSF

SPINED SPIDER (Family: Araneidae)

Clinging from the center of its web, the tropical spined spider might easily be mistaken for a wood chip, a flower, or some strange, exotic fruit. This short-legged spider relies on camouflage as well as its tough, leathery abdomen and colorful spines to discourage lizards, birds, and other predators from taking a spiky mouthful. But even sharp spines don't protect these spiders from wasps. Spider wasps sting their victims and carry the bodies back to line their nests. That way, wasp larva have plenty of spider bodies to eat.

Spined spiders use a special decoy to catch fly-eating insects. They decorate their web with little tufts of silk that look like tiny midge flies. When insects stop by for a "fly bite," they are trapped in the web instead.

Male spined spiders are pygmies compared to females. Small size comes in handy for males when they're courting and mating with short-tempered females—they're almost too small to be noticed, or eaten!

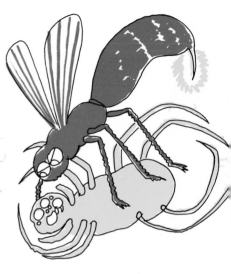

Wasps are dangerous to many spiders! Spider wasps are deadly to tarantulas; the big spiders hardly ever survive an encounter with this foe. This wasp crawls into a tarantula's burrow and stings the spider after a fierce battle—both rolling over and over. When stung, the spider is paralyzed. Alive but helpless, the giant spider is dragged to a grave dug by the wasp. The wasp deposits her egg inside the spider's abdomen and fills the grave with dirt. The spider may stay alive for months providing fresh food for the wasp larvae after they hatch.

SPIDERS

WANDERING SPIDER (Family: Ctenidae)

Wandering spiders do exactly that—they wander far from home to do their hunting. They are not attached to webs (like web weavers), and they don't rely on silk. In the past, some of these spiders—like the big orange wandering spider from the tropics of South America—have hitched rides to North America on banana boats, but these days new shipping methods discourage uninvited spider guests. In fact, many spider species have been transported from one place to another by humans. If they like the climate when they arrive, they often stay and raise families.

Another wandering spider, Phoneutria, from South American jungles, has a bite that's as bad as its bark. Hairy giants, these aggressive spiders look scary, and their powerful venom, acting on the nervous system, can be fatal.

The largest wandering spiders have a diet that includes frogs, lizards, mice, and even snakes. Of course, they don't say no to insects.

Many American Indian tribes view the wily spider with great respect. For the Dakotah, a perfect orb web symbolizes the heavens. In Pueblo myths of the Southwest, a spider created the first woman and the first man. In Cherokee folklore, a brave and tiny spider brought the gift of fire to the rest of the animals. Spider Woman gave the art of blanket- and basket-weaving to the Navajo.

Spiderman uses the skills of a spider to climb walls, jump from building to building, and trap the bad guys! This comic book superhero is now part of popular American folklore.

S P I D E R S

Good Sense

HAIRY MYGALOMORPH (Family: Theraphosidae)

Tarantulas are primitive spiders, which means they look a lot like their ancient ancestors. Around 360 million years ago, tarantula-like spiders crawled through swampy, steamy forests— the same forests that became today's coal supply for North America and Europe.

Because their fangs point "backward" under their body, tarantulas must throw themselves back and up to drive their fangs into prey. Although they strike with speed, getting ready can be a clumsy operation. More modern true spiders have fangs that are "cross-eyed." They can strike more efficiently without lifting their bodies up.

Legs are organs of touch for spiders, especially important for tarantulas because their eyesight is poor. They rely on touch—using their front legs and pedipalps—to find and capture prey. All spiders do have the ability to tell what tastes bad, sowbugs and stinkbugs, for instance, but not in the same way humans do. And while we have hairs in our nose and ears that help us smell and hear, spiders have hairs containing chemical receptors covering the *outside* of their bodies.

Some mygalomorphs are trap-door spiders—nifty critters that use the spines on their chelicerae as diggers to tunnel out bits of earth from their underground burrows. The earth is rolled into balls and carefully removed until the tunnel is complete. But these spiders are especially famous for their trap-doors—little hinged lids that fit tight to keep out rain and un-wanted visitors. Braced against the walls of their tunnels, trap-door spiders can hold the door so tightly shut that not even an arachnologist can force it open.

YUK STINK BUG!

34

SPIDERS

NURSERY WEB SPIDER (Family: Pisauridae)

Molting is a dangerous business for true spiders just like it is for tarantulas. This is the time they are most helpless and vulnerable to predators. This is also the time when spiders grow.

All eight legs begin lengthening as they're pulled from their old skeleton, or cuticle. Youngsters molt and lengthen their legs in less than 30 minutes, but older spiders may take as long as two hours. It isn't uncommon for spiders to get stuck inside their old cuticle. In that case, they will die. But if all goes well, the spider begins a series of "calisthenics" once the new legs are free. These exercises keep the spider's joints from stiffening.

After the nursery web spider completes its final molt (it could molt as many as 13 times!), it will be a mature adult ready to mate. The nursery web female is a wonderful mother. Her first job is to spin a silken cover over her eggs. Once complete, the mother totes her egg sac *everywhere* until the spiderlings emerge. The sac is attached to her chelicerae in front and moored with silk to her behind. After the spiderlings hatch, the female ties the sac to a bunch of leaves. Now she begins to remodel, pulling the leaves over with silk until she makes a very nifty "parachute." The mother hangs over the outside of this parachute nursery until her spiderlings are old enough to leave the nest.

Scientists have been studying spider's silk because it is such amazing stuff. They have even isolated the gene responsible for silk production. Some silk is sticky, some isn't. It's amazingly strong and flexible. Spider silk has even been used as cross-hairs in rifles.

Moths and butterflies rarely get stuck in a spider's web. That's because the scales on their wings are nonstick when it comes to spider silk.

SPIDERS

Photo, facing page, courtesy Animals Animals © G.I. Bernard/OSF

JUMPING SPIDER (Family: Salticidae)

This jumping spider is medium hairy as jumpers go. At home in tall grass and bushes, these primo hunters stalk and attack insects with great skill. Active in the daytime (which is very unusual for spiders!), jumping spiders use their big eyes to spot prey. (Perhaps it is all that sunshine that gives these friendly critters their bright and shiny decorations.) The keenest-eyed jumpers can see as far as twelve inches—a spider mile! With four pairs of eyes, each receiving a different-sized picture, jumping spiders can track motion from much longer distances. Once it spies its target prey, this spider creeps and crawls carefully forward until it is close enough to pounce.

Short and stout critters, jumpers are surprisingly graceful athletes. They run, dance, and leap with ease. Indeed, jumping spiders can leap more than forty times their own length. Using only a dragline to save them from falls (much as mountain climbers use a safety line), they fearlessly jump from leaf to leaf. In fact, they'll even jump off buildings to <u>catch</u> fly-by insects.

West African and West Indian myths tell many stories of the tricky spider, often a hero and sometimes the creator of the world. In European folklore, an itsy bitsy spider spun a web that hid the baby Jesus from enemy soldiers. Busy spiders also saved kings, queens, and Mohammed.

Photo, facing page, courtesy Animals Animals © M.A. Chappell

SPIDERS

SUN SPIDER (Family: Solpugidae)

When is a spider not a spider? When it's a sun spider—a close relative, but not a real spider. This arachnid has eight legs, just like spiders, as well as pedipalps and chelicerae. But it only sports two eyes, while most spiders have eight, or at least six.

In some ways, the sun spider might seem more like another arachnid, the scorpion. In fact, it is sometimes called a wind scorpion. But its pedipalps are not pincers, and it boasts no stinger.

It's not easy to figure out just who belongs where. For instance, the daddy longlegs spider isn't a spider. If you look at its body closely you may see lots of wrinkles but only one body part. There is no waist or obvious joint on a daddy longleg's body. Also, while spiders are usually solitary creatures, daddy longlegs often hang out in groups.

Unlike most spiders, Stegodyphus community spiders from southern Africa are groupies. They build, repair, and share an amazing web that can cover four yards square! Within their silken kingdom, community spiders use teamwork to handle flying ants, beetles, and grasshoppers (some are tens of times bigger than the spiders!) caught in the web. All Stegodyphus seem to share the work load, and the community spirit allows these spiders to maximize their hunting and spinning skills and to survive in a harsh environment. But a Stegodyphus web is not for commmity spiders alone. This micro-universe also houses lazy parasite spiders, wasp and moth larvae, and even a small mouse or two.

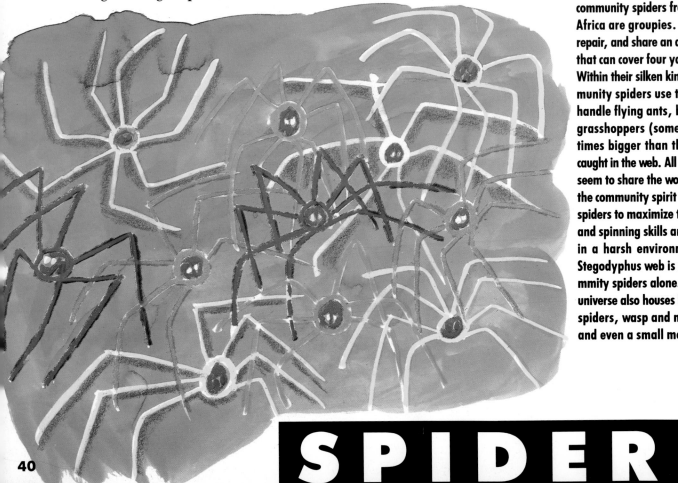

SPIDERS

BIRD-DROPPING SPIDER (Family: Thomisidae)

Three guesses what the bird-dropping spider looks like! This little crab spider is one of a group that protect themselves by looking like something no one wants to eat. Some are perfect imitations of tiny seeds, leaves, or flowers. But the Malaysian bird-dropping spider has one of the most unusual costumes of all, and it is especially convincing when perched on its web.

For spiders, camouflage works two ways—to discourage predators and to attract prey. When spiders are in disguise, predators like lizards, wasps, and birds may pass them by. But critters that spiders love to eat may think they see a bird dropping when it's really a hungry spider.

Another spider that sometimes imitates a bird dropping is the female bolas spider. This incredible huntress hangs by her back legs from a few strands of silk. With her front legs, she holds a silk line with a sticky blob at the end and waits for a moth to fly by. When her prey is within range, the bolas spider throws her silk line at the moth, "sticks it," and hauls it in to eat.

Australian Aborigines have long used a unique method of fly fishing. Poking the end of a pole into a sticky spider's web, the angler creates a long line of silk. This is dipped into the crushed body of a large silk spider. The rest of the spider's body and the fishing line are tossed into a stream where fish gather. As the fish bite at the scraps, their mouths are tangled in the silk and they are pulled to shore.

Photo, facing page, courtesy Animals Animals © OSF

SPIDERS

JUMPING SPIDER (Family: Salticidae)

Jumping spiders make their living as stalkers and hunters. With their strong eyes and powerful bodies, these brightly colored creatures rule the daylight hours as far as spiders go.

They spot their prey, creep slowly forward, and then pounce! But there are other jumping spiders who have discovered a different way of hunting —and a whole new look.

Ant mimics are jumping spiders, but they look just like ants. They have long and shiny brown bodies, and they even hold their front legs up like antennas and walk on six legs. This "act" allows them to mingle freely with ants. If you're wondering why, it may be because this way they can catch ants very easily. Another reason might be that ants don't taste good and many predators avoid them. Either way, these jumping spiders are great actors.

In the 1960s, scientists studying animal behavior used spiders and their webs for some unusual experiments. When a spider was fed a fly injected with caffeine, it spun a very "nervous" web. When spiders ate flies injected with the hallucinogenic drug, LSD, they spun webs of abstract and wild patterns. But spiders who were given sedatives fell asleep before they finished spinning. The webs were graphic examples of how these drugs affect both spiders and humans.

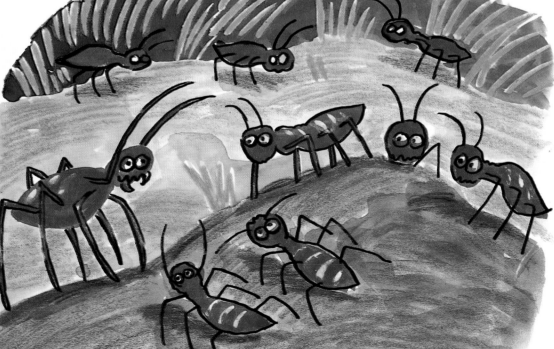

Recently, NASA launched a spider into orbit to see how its web-building skills worked in zero gravity. It only took the tiny spider three days to learn how to weave near-perfect webs in a weightless environment.

SPIDERS

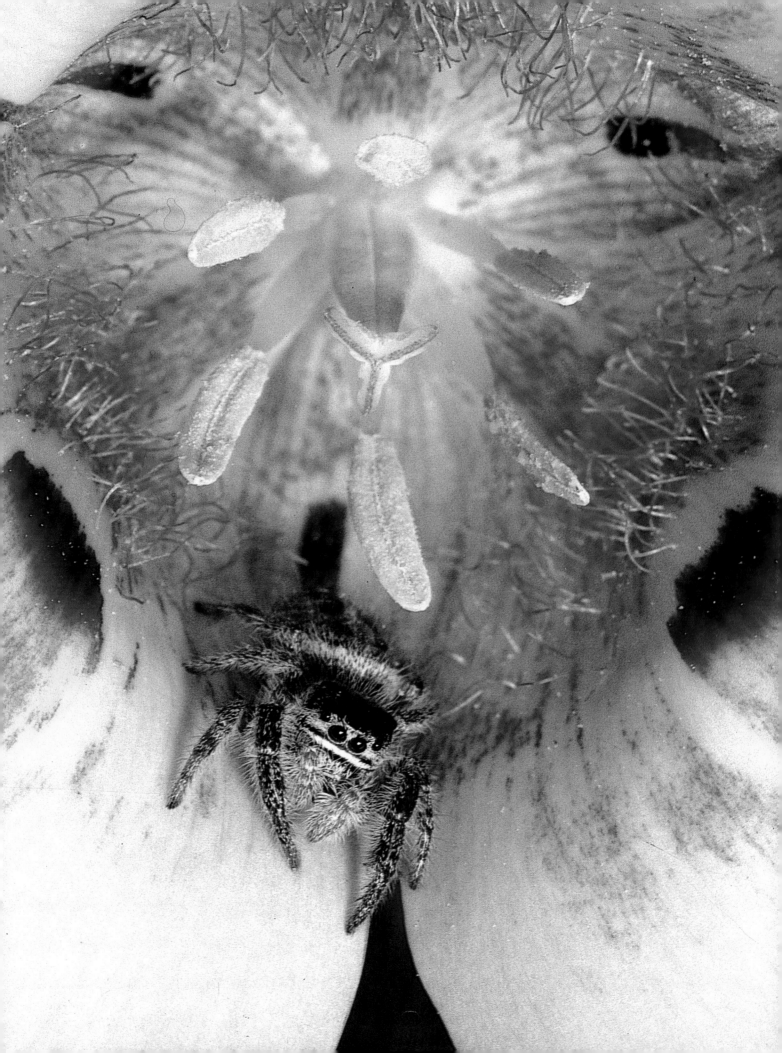

This glossarized index will help you find specific spider information. It will also help you understand the meaning of some of the words used in this book.

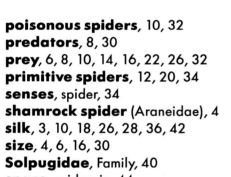

A huge spider that kills and eats rats (*Poecilotheria regalis*) (Neg. No. 313375; Courtesy Department Library Services, American Museum of Natural History)

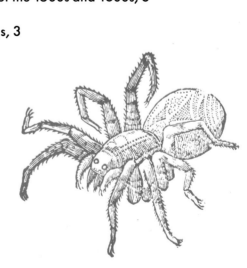

EXTREMELY WEIRD SERIES

*A*ll of the titles are written by Sarah Lovett, 8½" x 11", 48 pages, $9.95 paperback, $14.95 hardcover, with color photographs and illustrations.

Extremely Weird Bats
Extremely Weird Birds
Extremely Weird Endangered Species
Extremely Weird Fishes
Extremely Weird Frogs
Extremely Weird Insects
Extremely Weird Mammals
Extremely Weird Micro Monsters
Extremely Weird Primates
Extremely Weird Reptiles
Extremely Weird Sea Creatures
Extremely Weird Snakes
Extremely Weird Spiders

X-RAY VISION SERIES

*E*ach title in the series is 8½" x 11", 48 pages, $9.95 paperback, with color photographs and illustrations, and written by Ron Schultz.

Looking Inside the Brain
Looking Inside Cartoon Animation
Looking Inside Caves and Caverns
Looking Inside Sports Aerodynamics
Looking Inside Sunken Treasure
Looking Inside Telescopes and the Night Sky

THE KIDDING AROUND TRAVEL GUIDES

*A*ll of the titles listed below are 64 pages and $9.95 paperbacks, except for *Kidding Around the National Parks* and *Kidding Around Spain*, which are 108 pages and $12.95 paperbacks.

Kidding Around Atlanta
Kidding Around Boston, 2nd ed.
Kidding Around Chicago, 2nd ed.
Kidding Around the Hawaiian Islands
Kidding Around London
Kidding Around Los Angeles
Kidding Around the National Parks
 of the Southwest
Kidding Around New York City, 2nd ed.
Kidding Around Paris
Kidding Around Philadelphia
Kidding Around San Diego
Kidding Around San Francisco
Kidding Around Santa Fe
Kidding Around Seattle
Kidding Around Spain
Kidding Around Washington, D.C., 2nd ed.

MASTERS OF MOTION SERIES

*E*ach title in the series is 10¼" x 9", 48 pages, $9.95 paperback, with color photographs and illustrations.

How to Drive an Indy Race Car
 David Rubel
How to Fly a 747
 Tim Paulson
How to Fly the Space Shuttle
 Russell Shorto

THE KIDS EXPLORE SERIES

*E*ach title is written by kids for kids by the Westridge Young Writers Workshop, 7" x 9", and $9.95 paperback, with photographs and illustrations by the kids.

Kids Explore America's Hispanic Heritage 112 pages
Kids Explore America's African American Heritage 128 pages
Kids Explore the Gifts of Children with Special Needs 128 pages
Kids Explore America's Japanese American Heritage 144 pages

ENVIRONMENTAL TITLES

Habitats: *Where the Wild Things Live*
Randi Hacker and Jackie Kaufman
8½" x 11", 48 pages, color illustrations, $9.95 paper

The Indian Way: *Learning to Communicate with Mother Earth*
Gary McLain
7" x 9", 114 pages, two-color illustrations, $9.95 paper

Rads, Ergs, and Cheeseburgers: *The Kids' Guide to Energy and the Environment*
Bill Yanda
7" x 9", 108 pages, two-color illustrations, $13.95 paper

The Kids' Environment Book: *What's Awry and Why*
Anne Pedersen
7" x 9",192 pages, two-color illustrations, $13.95 paper

BIZARRE & BEAUTIFUL SERIES

A spirited and fun investigation of the mysteries of the five senses in the animal kingdom.

Each title in the series is 8½" x 11", $9.95 paperback, $14.95 hardcover, with color photographs and illustrations throughout.

Bizarre & Beautiful Ears
Bizarre & Beautiful Eyes
Bizarre & Beautiful Feelers
Bizarre & Beautiful Noses
Bizarre & Beautiful Tongues

RAINBOW WARRIOR SERIES

W hat is a Rainbow Warrior Artist? It is a person who strives to live in harmony with the Earth and all living creatures, and who tries to better the world while living his or her life in a creative way.

Each title is written by Reavis Moore with a foreword by LeVar Burton, and is 8½" x 11", 48 pages, $14.95 hardcover, with color photographs and illustrations.

Native Artists of Africa
Native Artists of North America
Native Artists of Europe

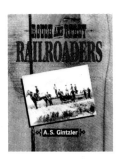

ROUGH AND READY SERIES

L earn about the men and women who settled the American West. Explore the myths and legends about these courageous individuals and learn about the environmental, cultural, and economic legacies they left to us.

Each title in the series is written by A. S. Gintzler and is 48 pages, 8½" x 11", $12.95 hardcover, with two-color illustrations and duotone archival photographs.

Rough and Ready Cowboys
Rough and Ready Homesteaders
Rough and Ready Loggers

Rough and Ready
 Outlaws & Lawmen
Rough and Ready Prospectors
Rough and Ready Railroaders

AMERICAN ORIGINS SERIES

M any of us are the third and fourth generation of our families to live in America. Learn what our great-great-grandparents experienced when they arrived here and how much of our lives are still intertwined with theirs.

Each title is 48 pages, 8½" x 11", $12.95 hardcover, with two-color illustrations and duotone archival photographs.

Tracing Our English Roots
Tracing Our French Roots
Tracing Our German Roots
Tracing Our Irish Roots

Tracing Our Italian Roots
Tracing Our Japanese Roots
Tracing Our Jewish Roots
Tracing Our Polish Roots

ORDERING INFORMATION
Please check your local bookstore for our books, or call 1-800-888-7504 to order direct from us. All orders are shipped via UPS; see chart below to calculate your shipping charge for U.S. destinations. **No P.O. Boxes please; we must have a street address to ensure delivery.** If the book you request is not available, we will hold your check until we can ship it. Foreign orders will be shipped surface rate unless otherwise requested; please enclose $3.00 for the first item and $1.00 for each additional item.

METHOD OF PAYMENT
Check, money order, American Express, MasterCard, or VISA. We cannot be responsible for cash sent through the mail. For credit card orders, include your card number, expiration date, and your signature, or call 1-800-888-7504. American Express card orders can be shipped only to billing address of card holder. Sorry, no C.O.D.'s. Residents of sunny New Mexico, add 6.25% tax to total.

Address all orders and inquiries to: John Muir Publications
P.O. Box 613
Santa Fe, NM 87504

(505) 982-4078
(800) 888-7504

For U.S. Orders Totaling	Add
Up to $15.00	$4.25
$15.01 to $45.00	$5.25
$45.01 to $75.00	$6.25
$75.01 or more	$7.25